TAKE-ALONG COMIC

GEMSTONE PUBLISHING

TIMONIUM, MARYLAND

STEPHEN A. GEPPI
President/Publisher and Chief Executive Officer

JOHN K. SNYDER JR.
Chief Administrative Officer

STAFF

LEONARD (JOHN) CLARK
Editor-in-Chief

GARY LEACH
Associate Editor

SUE KOLBERG
Assistant Editor

TRAVIS SEITLER
Art Director

SUSAN DAIGLE-LEACH
Production Associate

DAVID GERSTEIN
Archival Editor

MELISSA BOWERSOX
Director-Creative Projects

• IN THIS ISSUE •

ADVERTISING/ MARKETING

J.C. VAUGHN
Executive Editor

BRENDA BUSICK
Creative Director

JAMIE DAVID
Director of Marketing

SARA ORTT
Marketing Assistant

HEATHER WINTER
Office Manager
Toll Free
(888) 375-9800 Ext. 249
ads@gemstonepub.com

MARK HUESMAN
Production Assistant

MIKE WILBUR
Shipping Manager

RALPH TURNER
Accounting Manager

**ANGIE MEYER
JUDY GOODWIN**
Subscriptions
Toll Free (800) 322-7978

WALT DISNEY'S DONALD DUCK ADVENTURES 21
Take-Along Comic
November, 2006

Published by
Gemstone Publishing

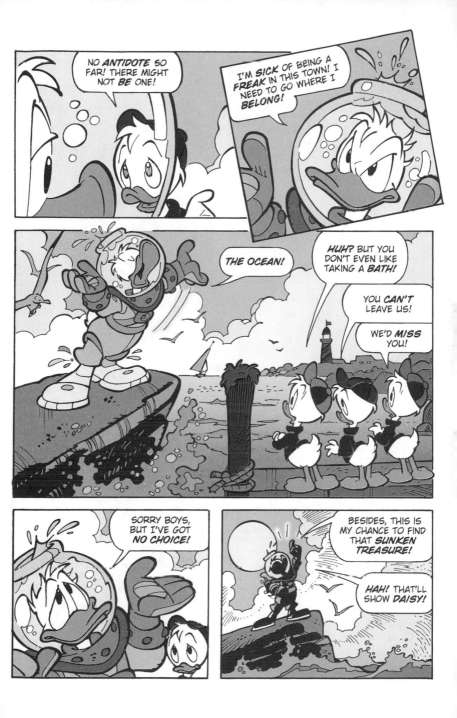

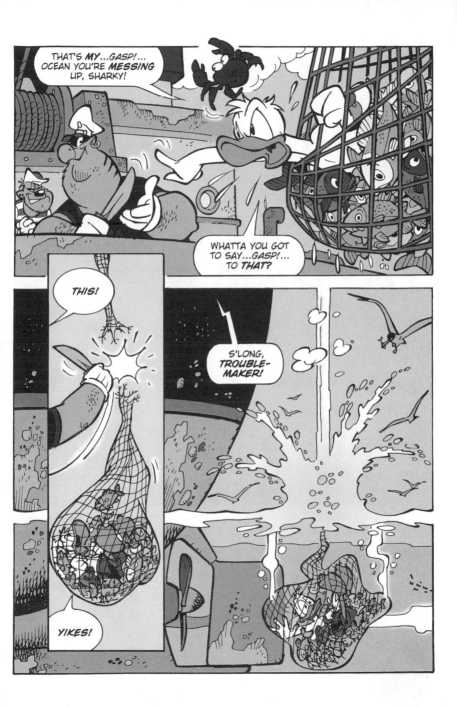

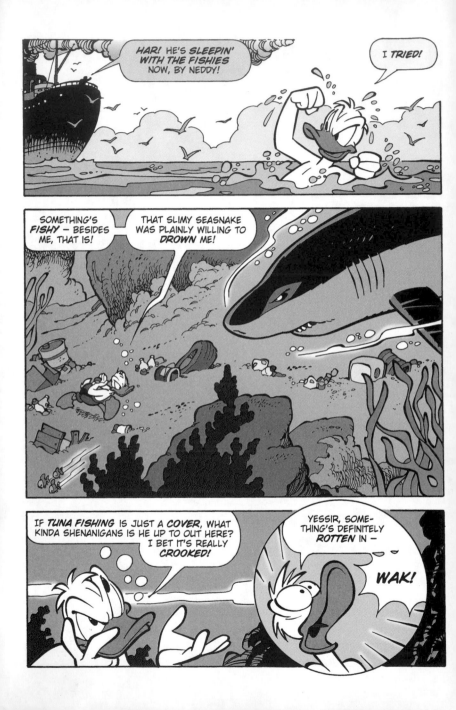

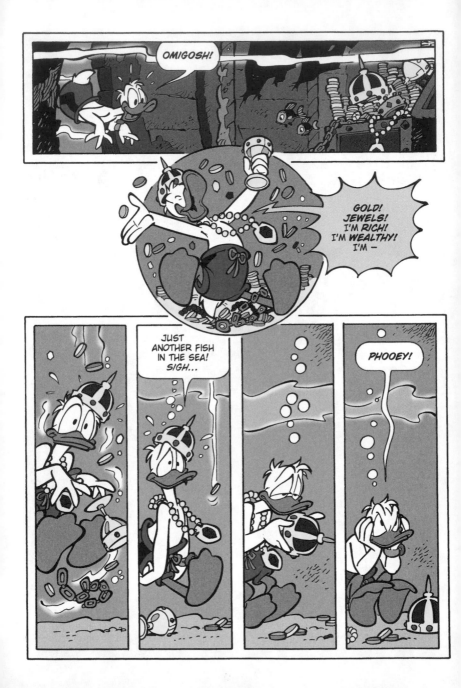

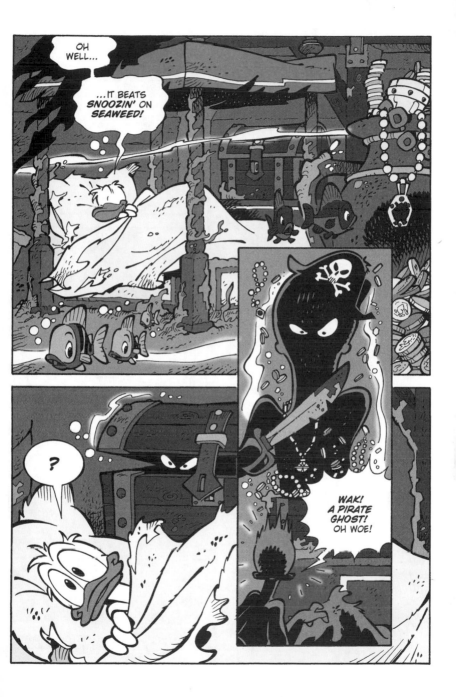

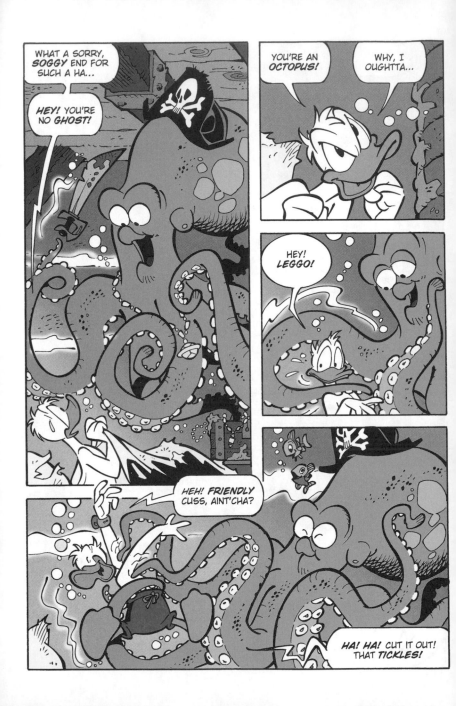

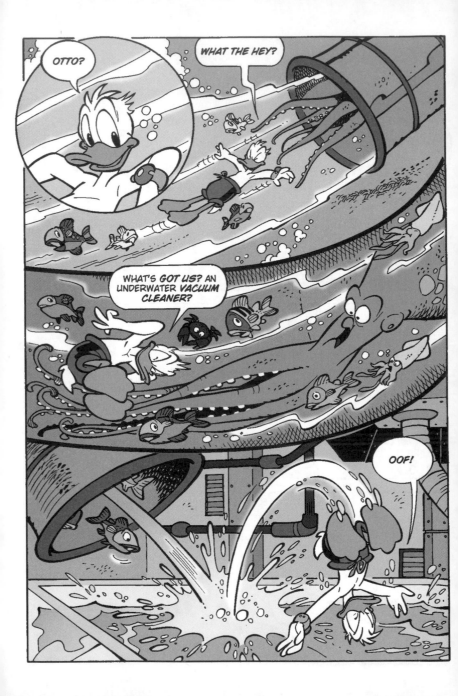

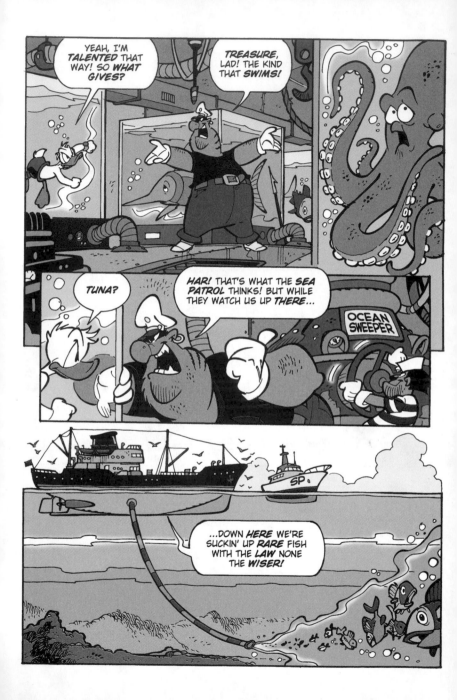

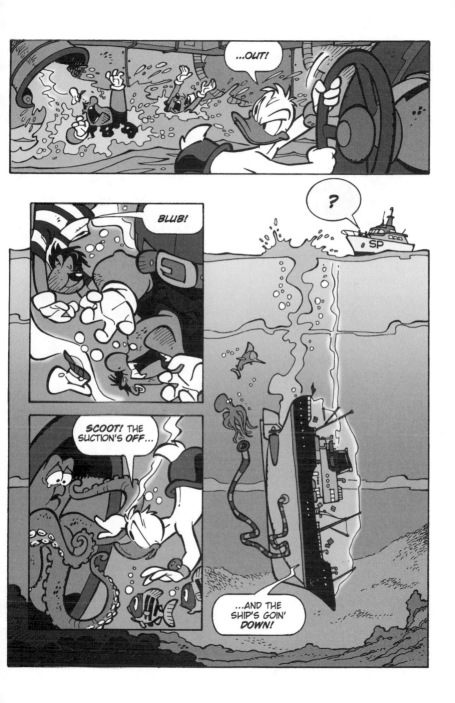

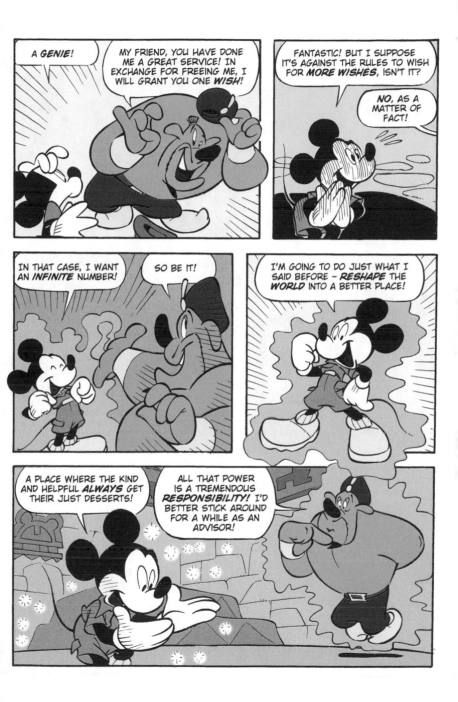

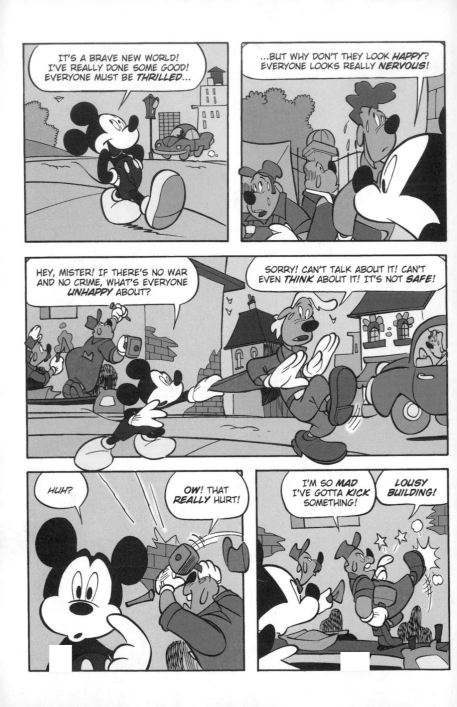

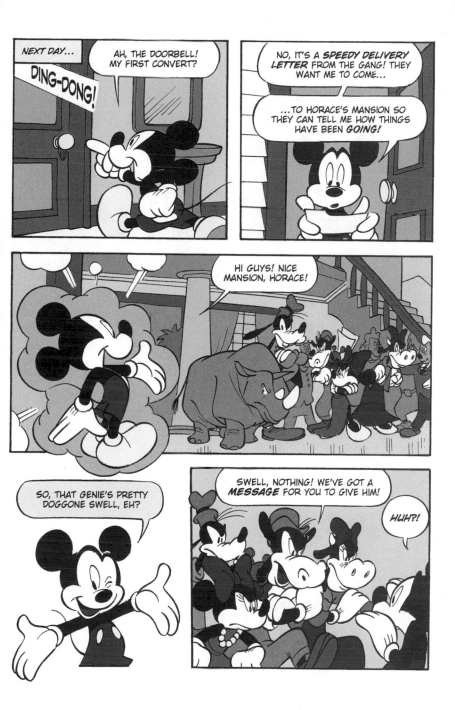

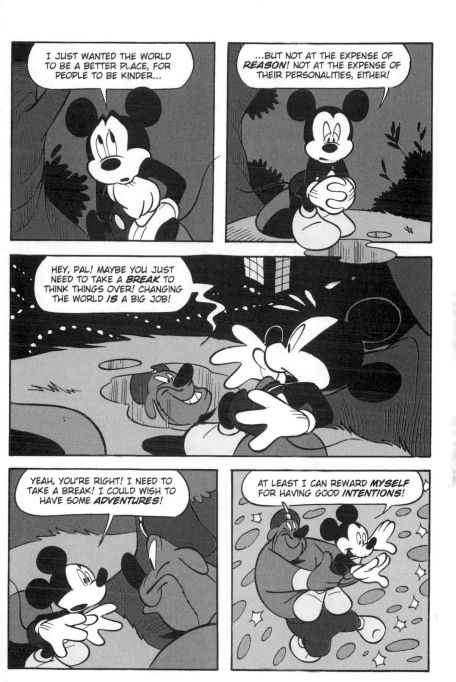

HAH! HE'S *LYING!* HE JUST WANTS WISHES FOR *HIMSELF!* DON'T YOU BELIEVE A WORD!

IT'S THE ONLY THING THAT MAKES *SENSE! YOU'RE* THE *LIAR*, GENIE!

ALL RIGHT! YOU *CAUGHT* ME!

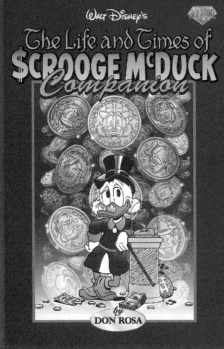

A DAY'S JOURNEY LATER...

DUCKBURG AHOY!

HA HA HA HA!

OH NO!

I CAN SEE BY YOUR FACE THAT YOU *FAILED!*

HRMPH!

IT'S NOT OVER YET!

I DON'T EVEN KNOW WHAT YOU WENT FOR, BUT I'M SURE IT HAD TO DO WITH OUR *BET!*

KEEP OPENING YOUR MOUTH AND YOU'LL HAVE TO EAT YOUR HAT!

HA HA!

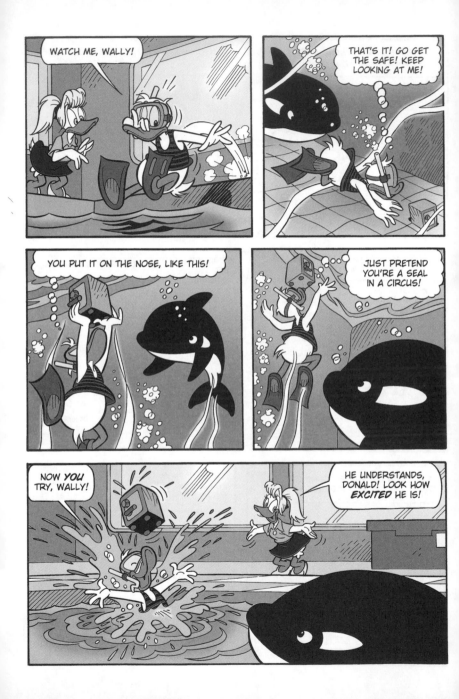

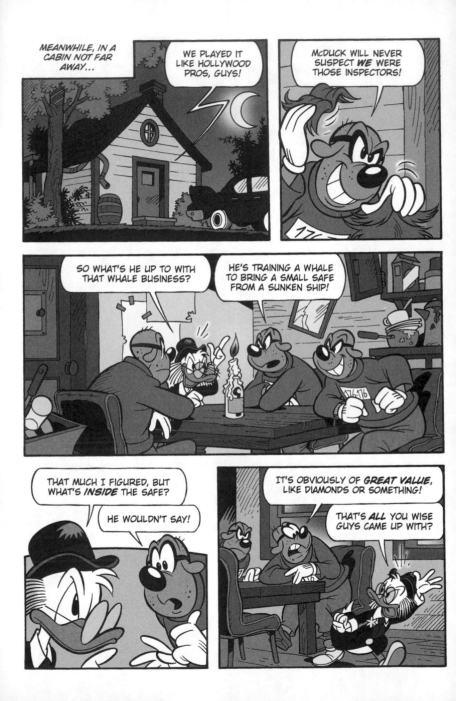

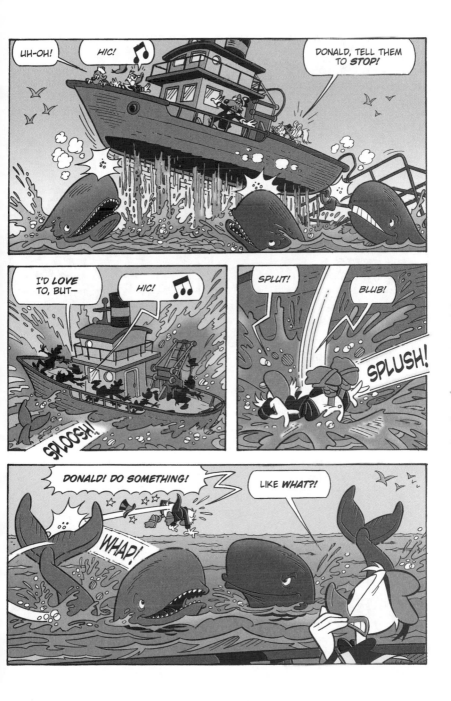

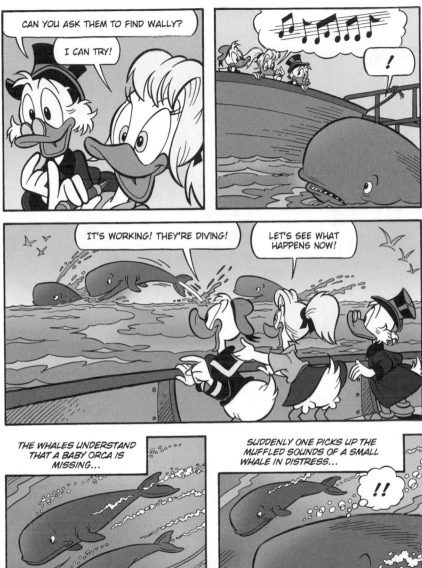

THE WHALES UNDERSTAND THAT A BABY ORCA IS MISSING...

SUDDENLY ONE PICKS UP THE MUFFLED SOUNDS OF A SMALL WHALE IN DISTRESS...

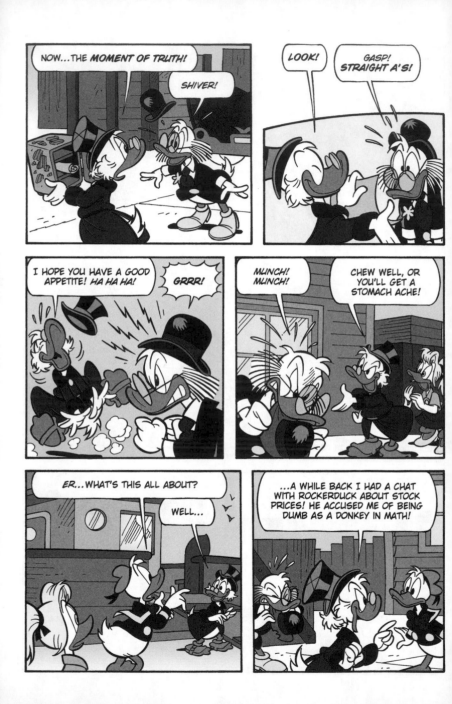